PLANNING AND FINANCING THE NEW CHURCH

By Martin Anderson

PUBLISHED BY

AUGSBURG PUBLISHING HOUSE
MINNEAPOLIS 15, MINNESOTA

PLANNING AND FINANCING THE NEW CHURCH
Copyright 1944
AUGSBURG PUBLISHING HOUSE

Printed and Manufactured in the United States of America by the
Augsburg Publishing House, Minneapolis 15, Minnesota

P R E F A C E

Planning and building churches is not the most important business of the Christian Church. "I will make you fishers of men," Jesus said. The quest for souls is our chief task. Yet making God's House beautiful, substantial and worthy of its high and holy purpose and meeting one's honest financial obligations, these are not matters of indifference.

Mistakes in design usually never can be corrected. They remain for a century or more. Errors in financing often are tragedies. They break the heart of the minister and make the church a source of anxiety to its members instead of joy and strength.

In the hope that it will enable churches to avoid errors in plan and financial procedure, to make the church a bit more conscious of church architecture and in the interest of better churches and sound financing, this treatise is written. It aims to give some guiding principles and suggestions. It is not technical. It is written for ministers, church committees, theological students and church members generally.

The writer makes no claim to have all knowlege or infallibility. But in our ministry in the providence of God it fell to our lot to help plan and finance three rather sizeable churches. We have served on other building committees. We have been given opportunities to travel in virtually all parts of the United States and in eight European countries. Everywhere we observed the chapels, churches, and cathedrals in which the people worshipped. We trust that our experience and opportunities for observation and study qualify us at least in a small way for the present task. What we have learned we gladly pass on to others. In the position which we now hold (District President) we frequently are asked for suggestions, especially by pastors with building programs before them, so we have decided to reduce to writing our thoughts regarding these matters.

Obviously what is written here must be adapted to local circumstances and situations. But the broad principles involved should be observed.

Very little is found in this treatise regarding the educational facilities of the church plan. Thereby we by no means intend to imply that this is unimportant. Every church should have child-centered and youth-centered programs. But this is another subject. For guidance here the reader must rely on other sources of information.

What is written here regarding financial procedures obviously also applies to debt reduction campaigns, remodeling or parish house projects.

The writer acknowledges his indebtedness to the writings of the Rev. F. R. Webber. We have been a diligent reader of his publication, "Lutheran Church Art," for many years. "The Small Church," a book by the same author, has been studied with much profit. Numerous articles appearing in the *Christian Herald* have been helpful. Material published by the Inter-denominational Bureau of Architecture, New York City, E. M. Conover, Director, has given valuable suggestions. Lastly, we acknowledge our indebtedness to Mr. Herbert A. Brand, Chicago, member of the American Institute of Architects, for his critical examination of Part One of this treatise.

MARTIN ANDERSON

C O N T E N T S

5

PART TWO... *Financing the New Church*

PART THREE... *Model Churches*

Gothic

•

Byzantine

•

Romanesque

•

Colonial

•

Modern

•

The Small Frame Church

•

Spanish

•

Log Churches

•

Remodeled Interiors

PART ONE

Planning the New Church

SHALL WE BUILD A NEW CHURCH?

Is There a Need?

Shall we build a new church? To answer this question we must first answer another: Is there a real need? Churches have been built that were not needed, often with tragic results. That the present church, if any, is old is no reason for building a new one if the old one is in a good state of repair and adequate for the requirements of the congregation. In Europe men point with pride to the great age of their churches. If a church is of good design it will never be out of date. That the present church is too small for the Easter and Christmas attendance is scarcely a reason for building a new and larger one. The better way is to add a service on these festival days if this can be done. To build mainly in order to have a more beautiful church is commendable, provided the congregation has the means, and provided the motives are love to God and zeal for His honor.

Being assured that there is a real need for a new building, another question arises: Is there need for the kind and size of structure which is contemplated? Many congregations have over-built, beyond their present or prospective needs and beyond their means. It is a rare congregation, in the cities at any rate, that has more than 50% of its members present on an average Sunday. It is folly therefore to build a church with seating capacity for its entire membership. When the church becomes crowded add another service. This can easily be done in parishes consisting of only one church. Roman Catholics provide as many masses as are required to make room for the people of the parish. It is a different matter if the pastor serves two or more congregations.

If there is a real need for the contemplated building program and the financial plan is sound then you may boldly and confidently ask both the Lord and your people to help. Then it is time to "rise up and build."

Authorization

The first step is to have the building project authorized by the congregation. This must be done at a legally called meeting, with a quorum present. A proper motion must be passed, a committee or committees must be elected and authorized to proceed with the project when building and financial plans have been approved by the congregation. *There must be no doubt about the proper authority for the building program.*

Organizing for the Task

In a congregation with a large membership two committees should be elected, a building committee and a building fund committee.

The function of the building committee is to select, or at least recommend, an architect, to plan the building, together with the architect, to advertise for bids and to open bids and decide upon the low bidders, to arrange details of contracts and to decide innumerable questions which will arise as the work proceeds. One building committee of which the writer was a member held eighty meetings.

The function of the building fund committee is to plan, prepare and conduct the building fund campaign, and to collect or supervise the collection of building fund contributions. A great deal more will be said about the work of this committee in a later chapter.

In a small congregation the two functions just outlined may be combined in one committee.

Choosing the Site

Usually the church site has to be selected. In choosing the site there are many considerations to be kept in mind. In the first place one must be sure that the lot has ample size. In the country or in villages this usually presents no difficulty as ground is inexpensive. In the city where ground values are high there is a tendency to acquire too little ground. You can build only on the ground which is yours and not on all of that. In many zones you are restricted to building on only a certain percentage of your lot. Then there usually is the building line. You must keep your structure back of this line. Some sections are zoned for residences only and a church cannot be built. One congregation bought a lot only to discover that it was in a section zoned for industrial purposes. Some day this church may have a boiler factory next door to it. There are restrictions as to materials to be used. In some zones you cannot build a frame structure. In many sections you must have a fire resisting roof. There are requirements as to the thickness of walls and foundations. There are these and many other restrictions and requirements. All should be investigated *before* the site is purchased.

For a small or medium size church plant the lot should be not less than 75x100 feet. 100x125 or 150 feet is much better. A large lot gives a better setting for the church and does not impose so many restrictions as to the type and plan of building to be constructed. A corner lot has several advantages. You are less restricted as to plan. You have more parking space and your church is more conspicuous and people can be more easily directed to it.

It is to be deplored that so often the plot is of absolute minimum size. Even if the design of the edifice is very good the effect is disappointing. The proper setting is lacking. Even a mediocre building in a fine setting of spacious lawns, with trees and shrubs, will be impressive.

Beware of restrictions in the deed to the site such as: "To be used for church purposes only." You likely will want to borrow money on your property and this can be done only with difficulty, if at all, with such a restriction. Or, you might change your mind and want to sell the lot. Again this restriction will stand in the way.

To discuss other community factors relating to the location of the church really lies outside of the purposes of this study, but we shall venture just a brief statement. In the city beware of a gift lot "on a nice quiet street." Put your church where the race of men passes by and be a friend of man. Choose a natural community center, perhaps near a school. If in a city make sure that there is good transportation, ascertain what racial or religious groups predominate in the community, study the anticipated growth of the neighborhood. The choice of a location is extremely important. The life of the church depends on a wise choice. "Better a poor building in a good location than a good building in a poor location." In a rural parish the choice of a location is far simpler, but here too seek to locate the church in a natural community center.

Choosing the Architect

The congregation must choose an architect to draw the plans and specifications for the new church. Lumber yard plans or plans drawn by some carpenter or contractor should be avoided for even the smallest church or chapel.

The building committee has no more important function than the selection of an architect. If a mistake is made in this selection there will be nothing but grief and regrets from first to last. If a wise choice is made the whole undertaking will be a delight and a never-ending satisfaction.

As a rule the charges of a good architect are no higher than those of a less competent one. In the end the incompetent man costs much more.

Architects' fees are about the same everywhere. The standard charge is 6% of the cost of the project, if supervision is included, and 4% or 4½% without supervision. Some competent architects work for a smaller fee, usually because they have a small office, with less overhead.

Choose an architect who has built good churches. Many will say that they are church architects who have made no special preparation for this type of work.

How should an architect be chosen? If the committee finds a man who has designed a number of churches of the historic and traditional type it usually is good judgment to engage him without any competition with other architects.

Another way is to invite a small number of architects who have designed good churches of the above mentioned type to submit sketches in a competition, the building committee to make the selection. However, many good architects will enter such a competition only on the condition that they receive a specified compensation for their work in case they are not given the commission. This is fair. The committee should be given authority by the congregation to spend a stipulated amount for this purpose. It will be money well spent. All sketches submitted by those not chosen should be returned at once to the architects who submitted them —otherwise you may be in difficulties about them later.

12

The American Institute of Architects has a set of rules for a competition which we shall not enter into here. This procedure is not often used except on very large projects.

We want to add a few words of warning in connection with the selection of the architect. Do not permit too many to submit preliminary sketches. It will only confuse the committee. Three or four, or at the most five, should be enough. Do not be misled by beautifully colored perspectives. Floor plans and elevations are much more reliable. Beware of engaging an architect because he happens to be somebody's uncle, nephew, brother-in-law or friend. Unfortunately, this sort of relationship does not necessarily qualify one for designing good churches.

only a glorified cellar. Often there isn't much glory in it. Usually it is damp and dark. It is limited in its use; there is no way in which it can add to the seating capacity of the church when there is an overflow attendance.

Moreover, basements cost much more than most folks realize. Usually a basement costs one-fourth of the total cost of the structure. Included in this cost are such items as: Excavation, extra wall construction, gravel or ash fill, a thick concrete slab, waterproofing, wood floor, plaster on walls and ceilings, partitions, doors, windows, casements, area-ways, hardware and paint.

The money spent for a basement will go a great way toward building a parish house unit above ground. A full basement is justified only if the means are very limited and the cost of additional ground is prohibitive, or if additional ground is not available. The trend at the present time is away from basements. Usually the better way is to excavate for the heating plant and lavatories only.

The alternative to a basement is a parish house unit built on top of the ground. If desired this can be so placed that it can add to the seating capacity of the church in case of an overflow attendance. The parish house has the greater advantage of being light and airy; it makes for a more elastic plan; it adds to the mass and the attractiveness and impressiveness of the plant. Basement classrooms are banned in all public schools. Why should not the church have the same high standards for its schools?

When means are limited it may become necessary to build in units. The old way was to build the basement and stop with that until more funds were available. Such a basement, without its superstructure is an unsightly thing. Yet, many congregations have had to remain in such uninteresting quarters for a long time. How much better, then, to build the first unit of the sanctuary-parish house plant. It is above ground, it is attractive, it is complete. Let the first unit be the parish house if that seems advisable. It combines facilities for worship, education and fellowship.

Building Gradually

If funds are limited do not try to finish everything at once. The American way is to do things in a hurry. In Europe men have taken five hundred years to build a cathedral. The interior may well be finished one step at a time; altar, pulpit, font, pews, light fixtures, floor covering, lectern, organ, stained glass windows may be added gradually—over a period of years, if necessary. Temporary equipment may well be used while the funds are being accumulated for permanent equipment. This has several advantages. The structure looks right from the outside; it almost invariably means better equipment; it keeps the congregation interested and working; it saves paying interest on borrowed money.

In England many churches have been built on such an installment plan. First the main section of the nave was built, next the chancel, then another bay or two; then one transept, later the other, finally the tower. Thus each part can be built well and a heavy indebtedness avoided. In such a procedure it is extremely important that the nave be set in the right place on the plot.

If a basement is included in the plan this may be excavated but left unfinished until means are available.

Materials

The material of which the church is built may be either stone, brick with stone trim, brick without stone trim, brick veneer, cement blocks, or wood. Any of these may well be used. They are not equally good, but any of these materials will do.

Stone, of course, is the best. In some localities the cost of stone is not much higher than the cost of brick. Therefore it is well to take alternate bids on stone and brick.

Brick with not too much stone trim is always good. But do not overdo the stone trimming. Many brick structures are overloaded with cut stone trim. This adds too much to the cost and makes the church look fussy. There are so many ways of laying brick that an all brick church can be made to look very interesting and attractive.

Much of the effect in a brick structure will depend upon the treatment of the mortar joints. These may vary both in form, width and color. The width may be from ⅛ inch to ½ inch. The joints may be flush with the wall or grooved. Sometimes they are made V-shaped. The color may be white, gray, buff, chocolate, or black. However, not all colors are suitable for a church. The same brick laid up in various widths, shapes and colors of mortar joints will appear very different. The proper treatment of the joints adds character and interest.

A brick veneer job well done can be very satisfactory. If ordinance restrictions forbid building of wood and funds are not sufficient to build of solid masonry there is nothing else to do but to choose brick veneer.

Cement blocks are not at all attractive, but make a substantial job.

Wood is an excellent material of which to build and with proper year by year maintenance a wood church will stand for several hundred years. A well designed frame structure is perfectly honest and can be made lovely. But do not try to imitate a masonry building with pointed windows and arches, sham buttresses and the like. Pointed windows and arches in a wooden structure are not in the best taste. These belong to masonry. You do not need these to make the building look like a church, if otherwise the design is churchly.

Cobblestones or "niggerheads" are a legitimate material to use in a locality where these are found. Some very interesting chapels and churches have been made of this material.

Logs may be used with good results for a chapel or a small church. A fine example of this is Grace Lutheran Church, Sandy Lake, near McGregor, Minnesota. (See cut in Part Three of this treatise.)

Artificial or manufactured stone which sometimes has been used for trim, window tracery, copings and buttress caps, has not been found very satisfactory. Often it has to be repaired or replaced after exposure to the changing weather conditions.

Stone should never be painted either on the interior, as in window tracery, or on the exterior of a building. Neither ought brick to be painted. If necessary to preserve it there are oil treatments that may be used instead of paint.

Relation of Size to Cost

An important fact to be borne in mind is that the main factor in the cost of any structure is its size. Every cubic foot of content represents a definite item of cost. You cannot add a foot to the length or width of your structure, you cannot add a porch or an entrance way, or a little side room of some kind, without adding a corresponding amount to the price. Other factors enter in. One church may be much more ornamental and elaborate than another. But by and large this is true: The size determines the cost.

Therefore, the committee should ask the architect to state the number of cubic feet in the whole structure, or in any part of it under consideration. The architect or some contractor familiar with this type of construction can give the approximate cost per cubic foot. The cost varies in different localities and at different times, depending on labor conditions and the like. But, in normal times, the cost usually runs from 30 cents to 40 cents per cubic foot in the case of masonry and less for wood construction. This price has reference to a fully completed and equipped church.

To estimate the approximate cost of the contemplated structure, compute the number of cubic feet enclosed within the building, using outside measurements, starting 6 inches below footings and figuring up to half of the height of the gable. To keep down costs you must keep down size.

Acoustics

Good acoustics is extremely important. In a small church or chapel there usually is no problem. In a large church acoustical conditions sometimes are very bad. The obtainment of good acoustics no longer is guess work. It is an exact science. No architect should be engaged who is not thoroughly conversant with this subject. While an adequate amount of soft surfaces is the main requisite for good acoustics there also are other factors. It is a church architect's business to understand this. If the architect engaged is not familiar with this subject insist that he employ a consultant who is an expert in this field.

Storage Space

Among the items frequently overlooked by building committees is provision for adequate storage space, particularly space for the storage of dining room tables. The result often is that tables and other articles too numerous to mention are found here and there throughout the whole structure, making the church look messy and unkempt.

Sound Construction

The final word on the functional aspects of the new church plant is: Make sure the building is structurally sound, solid and strong. Beware of flimsy construction. See that footings and foundations are ample in view of soil conditions. Do not skimp on the thickness of the walls. See that walls and roofs are adequately braced. Many churches have fallen down in ordinary windstorms or because of a heavy snow load.

Constant expense is the price paid for shoddy construction. There are ways of saving money at the outset by using inferior materials and flimsy construction, but you pay for it later. Good construction and good materials mean low maintenance.

Do not build at all unless you have means enough to make the structure safe. In building, as in everything else, you usually get what you pay for, no more. The writer visited a comparatively new church recently with great cracks in the masonry everywhere and unsightly tie rods to keep the structure from spreading. The reason? Too little money provided to do the job right.

In this connection do not be afraid of a few pillars in the church, as in aisle and clerestory construction. Pillars are structurally sound and symbolically desirable. They suggest strength and permanence. What if a few people must sit behind the pillars on Easter Sunday? They will come again the next Sunday and come a bit earlier. Most people like to go where there are crowds.

Do not try to get marked down prices on materials and equipment. Pay the just market price for everything. Do not make the church look cheap in the eyes of the world by asking for concessions in price on every hand.

THE ARTISTIC AND ECCLESIASTICAL CONSIDERATIONS

Distinctiveness

The House of God must be distinctive; it must be at once recognizable as a church. The exterior design must indicate, even to the most casual observer, that this is not an auditorium, a theatre, a post office or a library, but a church.

A tower, perhaps with a spire, helps to identify the structure as a church. Towers may be put in various places: At the front of the church in the center; in one of the front corners; at the point where the parish house connects with the church; at the crossing of the nave and the transepts. The tower may even be set apart from the main structure of the church as a campanile. If there is a spire, always it should be surmounted by the cross. The cross more than anything else identifies the edifice as a Christian church.

If means are lacking for a tower, a flèche may be used. This is less expensive than a tower and is distinctively ecclesiastical.

But if the means are lacking for a tower, a flèche or bell cove, in any event let there be a cross at the peak of the front gable.

A tower can be much more than an expensive ornament. We know of a church in which the tower is utilized on five levels: The basement level is a rest room; the first floor is the entrance to the parish house; the second is the pastor's study; the third is a class room; the fourth is the belfry.

Finally let the approaches and the entrances be such that they seem to say to every wayfarer: Come in! Welcome!

The interior, too, must be distinctive. It must be infinitely more than an auditorium or a hall. All that one sees within the sanctuary must seem to say: "This is the House of God, this is the gate of heaven."

The altar must have the undisputed place of honor in the sanctuary. It must be the main focal point. All the lines of the church, the windows, pillars or pilasters, must carry the eye forward to the altar. Everything must converge there. Nothing must obstruct the view, neither pulpit, lectern, organ console nor choir. Nothing must compete with the altar for the chief place of honor.

The writer is a Lutheran pastor. That which makes a church Lutheran is not that it is Gothic, Romanesque, Colonial or Modern, but that the altar is given its rightful place of honor and that the pulpit and baptismal font are properly placed. We stress the three means of grace in the designing and arrangement of the church as well as in its teachings.

It follows from what has just been said that the chancel must be of ample size. It must be more than a niche. It need not be one-third of the total length of the structure as some advocate, but it should be sufficiently roomy to give the right setting for the altar.

A properly designed and equipped church intensifies the mood for worship. There is something about it that even when you enter alone a voice seems to say: "Let us pray." It has been said of many a church that you do not need a minister leading the service; you worship instinctively. The whole atmosphere calls to worship and seems to say: "The Lord is in His holy temple, let the whole earth keep silence before Him." A sermon is preached in this sacred silence. Unconsciously almost the mind slips from the temporal to the eternal, from the material to the spiritual. Such a church speaks the language of eternity and leads men to say, "We look not to the things that are seen but to the things that are not seen, for the things which are seen are temporal, the things which are not seen are eternal." Such a church heightens the desire to preach well and worship well. It calls forth the best in human hearts. It brings the mood and attitude for worship.

Beauty

The House of God must be beautiful, as beautiful as we know how to make it. More or less the love of beauty is found in every heart. The church should be the most beautiful house in the community. The Lord Himself designed one church, Solomon's temple. It was the most magnificent place of worship the world has ever seen. "Because she has been forgiven much she loveth much." In gratitude for God's

22

pardoning grace we should consecrate to His honor and service the very best that we can do in wood, brick or stone, only wishing that it might be a thousand times better. When we seek to beautify the House of God there usually are those who raise the cry: "Why this waste?" But they have Judas for their example. For often the good costs no more than the inferior. Beauty is not so much a matter of price as of good design and good taste.

Everything that is cheap, gaudy or tawdry should be rejected. Fussy ornamentation should be ruled out. The church should not be "cozy" or "pretty," but pleasing and inviting and withal be characterized by a noble dignity. A man said: "I like a church with a smiling face." While it is true that the church is a place for the penitential tear and a cry out of the depths, "God be merciful to me a sinner," it also is the House of Gladness. "I was glad when they said unto me, Let us go into the house of the Lord," the Psalmist said. It is above all a place where glad tidings shall be proclaimed, a place where the love of God shines through. It is a place where fears are dispelled and despondence departs. A sense of trust and confidence settles upon the soul.

Here man and God meet face to face. To souls that have cried, "Oh, that I knew where I might find Him" will be proclaimed:

> "Here bring your wounded hearts,
> Here tell your anguish;
> Earth hath no sorrow that Heaven cannot cure."

The man who has been groping and feeling after God will discover that God has been on a quest for him with a love that will not let him go.

> "Bells still are chiming and calling,
> Calling the young and old to rest,
> But above all the soul distressed,
> Longing for rest everlasting."

The chief attraction of the House of God is the Christ Who comes to us through Word and sacrament. And Word and sacrament have the same efficacy in lowly shanty or cathedral. Yet should we not seek to make the building consecrated to such high and holy purposes as beautiful as we know how to make it! When the motives are gratitude to God and zeal for His honor, who will say that there is not spiritual beauty in such a task?

H I S T O R I C T Y P E S

Evaluating the Achievements of the Past

In planning the new church have respect for the historic and the traditional. Do not despise or ignore values that have been discovered and developed through many generations of consecrated study and toil. You probably are not qualified to improve much on the work of the past.

Study the accumulated knowledge of centuries. Church architecture and ecclesiastical art are as much a special field as medicine and dentistry. Snap judgments by those who have not made even a superficial study in this field and the opinions of those who perhaps have not read a single book or even a good article on the subject have no value.

The pastor in particular and as far as possible the members of the building committee, should read a few good treatises on church art and architecture. Until you do, don't trust your opinions and conclusions too much.

What can happen when those with no knowledge of this field attempt to plan a church is illustrated by this incident: A pastor conceived the idea that the new church, seating about 300, should be like Solomon's temple. The pillars are there and a few details mentioned in the Old Testament description, but as may be imagined, the result was atrocious.

There are especially three historic types of architecture in common use among us, the Gothic, the Romanesque and the Colonial. All are good. But whatever type is chosen, be consistent; stick to it. Something in a design may be beautiful, but out of place. Do not have Gothic windows, and a Romanesque ceiling and Romanesque arches. It is true that the Gothic does permit some variations; the other types do not. In Gothic, for instance, you may have a transept on one side of the edifice and the tower on the opposite side. Nothing similar to this can be done in Romanesque or Colonial.

The Gothic

The Gothic type has been most extensively used in American churches, particularly among Protestants. It has much in its favor. "Forever upwards ascend the lines of the Gothic spirit." But it takes more than a few pointed arches and windows to make a church Gothic. There must be length, and the right relation of width, length and height. "Gothic is not a matter of surface ornament; it is a structural system." For a fine discussion of Gothic churches see the writings of Ralph Adams Cram.

The Romanesque

The Romanesque style has been used extensively among Protestants as well as Roman Catholics. It is characterized by the round arch, barrel vault, and massiveness of the structure. Horizontal lines are emphasized, whereas in the Gothic style it is the perpendicular lines that are made to stand out.

The Colonial

The Colonial type of architecture is much more distinctively American than the Gothic or Romanesque. It took its inspiration from the Georgian, used extensively in England. The immortal Sir Christopher Wren, designer of St. Paul's in London, is among the chief exponents of the Georgian. No one ever surpassed him in designing beautiful towers and spires.

Colonial churches are built of wood or brick. They are rectangular in shape. If built of wood the structure is always to be painted white; if of brick the exterior woodwork is painted white. Interior woodwork and chancel furniture are painted white. Pews are white with dark top rail. Pew ends are low and square and rectangular in shape. (Avoid the arm chair pew end in any type of church). Clear glass may be used in windows, the panes being 9 inches by 12 inches or smaller. Window heads may be square or semi-circular. A tall, light and graceful spire, with two or three or four diminishing stages will add charm to the Colonial church.

The Colonial type fits a modest budget. Savings can be made in the item of millwork, as good standard window trim, doors and so forth, are on the market, thus avoiding the necessity of having these items made special. There are also other savings in this style.

The Spanish

The Spanish type may be used, especially in certain localities, as for instance in California. It would not be good judgment to use the Spanish type in sections of the country to which it is altogether foreign.

The Modern

What about the Modernistic type? It can be made very beautiful. If the chancel with altar and pulpit is given the right treatment there is no reason why this type of architecture cannot be used. But as yet it does not have the hallowed associations of the older types.

If the modern style is used it must express the functions of a church. The edifice must look like a church, not like an exposition building, an industrial building or a club house. The design must be ecclesiastical to the extent that even a child will recognize it as a church. Some attempts at designing churches in this style have been failures from this point of view.

The modern is a less expensive style than some others. It omits all parts that are not functional. All applied ornaments are pared off. This tends to reduce the cost.

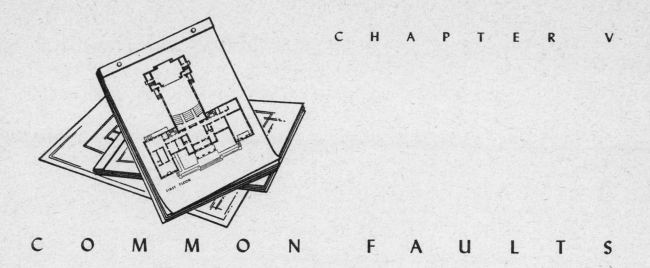

CHAPTER V

COMMON FAULTS

The Auditorium Type

At least until recently the most common offense against good design has been the square auditorium or theatre type of church. Often the pulpit is put in one corner and circular seating is installed. The altar, if any, is placed in a little niche behind a lectern type of pulpit. The entire arrangement suggests a lecture type of hall and not a church.

As a rule, these churches have no center aisle, a drawback in any church. Let there be a long aisle pointing up to the altar, with the opening in the communion rail in the center, not at the side. This emphasizes the length of the church and tends to accentuate the altar. Moreover, a center aisle is more convenient for weddings, funerals and processions.

Keeping the church somewhat long and narrow, not only makes for more graceful lines, it also reduces the cost, by making the span narrower. The wider the span the greater the cost, even if the size of the church be no greater.

The nave in European cathedrals is extremely narrow in proportion to the great length of these edifices. There, no doubt, are several reasons for this: One reason is structural. There was no steel for trusses in the days when these were built. In the second place the great emphasis was on the liturgy, not on preaching. With steel available, and with the right place given to preaching, we should be able to strike a happy medium.

It has been gratifying to note that in recent years even among denominations in which the meeting house or square auditorium type of church long was popular, there has been a definite trend to the traditional and historical types. The chancel is included in the plan with an altar instead of a communion table and a pulpit instead of a lectern.

Sloping Floors

Another fault, which happily is disappearing, is the sloping floor. The sloping floor also suggests a theatre instead of a church. It is proper that the congregation wants to see as well as hear the minister as he officiates at the altar, and wants to see the wedding party. But this can be accomplished by raising the chancel floor. It can be from three to seven steps above the floor of the nave, depending on the size of the edifice. A raised chancel floor is the alternative to a sloping floor in the nave.

Crowded Chancels

The common error of making the chancel too small and crowded already has been noted. It is mentioned again only for emphasis. Making the chancel too deep, as advocated in some quarters, is open to several objections. Notably two: It adds too much to the cost; it makes too great a separation between the officiating clergyman and the congregation. The more common error, however, is to make the chancel too small.

Note: Some denominations distinguish between chancel and sanctuary, the sanctuary designating only that part where the altar is placed. As used here, chancel designates the entire raised part in the front of the interior of the church. The word sanctuary also is used to designate the entire part of the church plant which is set aside for worship.

Concerning Choir Lofts

Where to put the choir is a troublesome question for most building committees. A divided choir placed in the chancel is the solution in some denominations. But this arrangement is open to objection, especially if the choir marches to the front of the chancel to sing its anthems. This is a disturbing factor in the service and suggests a concert rather than a worship service.

Placing the choir in a gallery at the rear of the church has much in its favor. This is almost a universal practice in European churches and in Roman Catholic churches everywhere. If the choir is placed in the gallery the organ also ought to be there.

Under no circumstances should the choir be placed behind or above the altar. No matter by whom this has been done, no matter how often it has been done, it is wrong! It detracts from the altar and disturbs the congregation.

Nor should the choir be placed on a high platform in one corner of the church with seats facing the congregation. It disturbs the worship both for congregation and choir and detracts from the appearance of the church.

It is impossible to be very specific about the place of the choir because churches are so different in size and plan. But the guiding principle must be this: Put the choir where it will not be too conspicuous, where it will be heard rather than seen.

The location of the choir has a direct bearing on the location of the organ. The choir and organ should be in close proximity for best musical and liturgical results. By all means do not have a lot of exposed organ pipes, real or imitation, behind the altar. If the organ must be back of the altar, use a grill and keep the pipes out of sight.

Concerning Organs

Regarding organs, we are constrained to say that too much money often is put into an instrument. Put your money into getting a good organist, rather than into a big organ.

Electric organs are of doubtful virtue. In the opinion of this writer, it is far better to get a good pipe organ than an electric organ of comparable cost. If space and funds are extremely limited, one might justify the purchase of an electric organ, but scarcely otherwise.

Concerning Windows

Windows have been made too large in many churches. This is first of all a question of scale, of right proportion. Windows need not be large to admit sufficient light if they are placed high enough in the wall. Besides, there is such a thing as having too much light. There is a certain richness in stained glass, and a certain mystical and devotional atmosphere, which you cannot have with strong, glaring light. No money is saved by having large openings, because good mullions and good stained glass are expensive.

Avoid opalescent glass. Avoid large picture windows; they rarely are well done. Rather use small medallions, artistically executed, surrounded by good stained glass in geometric design, and rich in color. If means are not available for stained glass, ordinary tinted glass of geometric design and leaded makes windows that are churchly as well as pleasing.

Concerning Ceilings

In some churches the ceiling is made much too dark. Exposed trusses, purlins and rafters can make a beautiful ceiling. But they must not be finished too dark. It makes the building seem top heavy and the whole interior somewhat dingy. Use a moderately dark stain and brighten up the trusses and purlins with good stencil work. If the stenciling is done before the trusses are lifted into place the cost will not be great. The result in giving life and brightness to the ceiling will be most gratifying.

A ceiling with stained roof planks, rafters, trusses and purlins has many advantages. It seldom leaks; it never needs to be redecorated; there is no danger of falling plaster; it is acoustically good. Such a ceiling treatment is suited especially to a Gothic church. Its appropriateness in other styles will be questioned by many.

In recent years there has been a tendency to use various types of composition material instead of plaster. There are many such on the market. With moderation this material can be used, especially for ceilings. If it is not overdone it improves the acoustical conditions. Covering both walls and ceiling with such material makes the church acoustically too dead. There is too much sound absorption. Besides, this usually is not a very durable material. It may bulge and buckle and pull loose from the wall. If placed on the lower portion of the wall it will not stand the wear.

Concerning Spires

Spires apparently are difficult to design well. There are a great many spires of poor design throughout the country. Many of them are chubby and lacking in grace. Others abruptly become spindly and suggest a tooth pick or an oil can. In studying the proposed spire for your church do not be misled by a perspective drawing. Study the elevations. Better far a good tower without a spire, something which seems to be more easily designed, than a spire lacking in grace and good proportions.

Miniature Cathedrals

In some quarters there has been a tendency to build cathedrals in miniature. Thus, the aisle and clerestory construction has been used in quite small churches. This is not good judgment. Likewise transepts in a small church are not good. They are meant for larger edifices. Instead one may have a gable on either side of the building with a little offset in either wall. This makes for interest in the design. Instead of a chancel arch many a small church would look better with a rood beam to define the chancel.

Concerning Interior Decoration

Gaudy interior decoration should be avoided. Let there not be too many bright colors and numerous bands, borders, dadoes, and scrolls. A restful interior that gives a feeling of repose should be the aim.

On the other hand, pews and other woodwork, as noted before, should not be stained too dark. A too dark treatment makes the church seem dead and gloomy. There always is a happy medium.

Imitations

Beware of imitations. Paint and plaster are good, honest materials. But do not try to paint the plaster to make it look like stone. Do not paint wooden columns to simulate marble. Plaster is an honest material. Why paint it and stripe it in an effort to make it look like something else? Imitation beams and columns, painted on plaster, are nothing short of ridiculous. Compo board arranged to simulate stone belongs in the same category. Sham buttresses made of light wood framework, lath and plaster, which are not load bearing and are structurally meaningless and superfluous, do not belong to honest construction. Buttresses are for strength and not for ornament.

Electric lights on the altar made to look like candles, is another example of imitation. Artificial flowers on the altar are out of place. Dummy organ pipes designed to camouflage a small organ to make it seem much larger are a case in point.

Everything in the House of God must be sincere, honest and genuine. "God is a spirit and they that worship Him must worship in spirit and truth." The place of worship as well as the worshiper must be characterized by sincerity and truth. We plead for honesty in building and equipping the House of God.

Remodeling

Poorly designed and equipped churches may sometimes be remodeled quite successfully. Many barn-like structures and churches of the auditorium type, have been made churchly and beautiful. A few suggestions regarding remodeling will be found in the final section of this treatise.

The Long View

In concluding this section of our treatise we can do no better than to quote these famous words of John Ruskin:

"When we build let us think that we build for ever. Let it not be for present delights, nor for present use alone, let it be such work as our descendants will thank us for, and let us think . . . . that a time is to come when these stones will be held sacred because our hands have touched them, and that men will say as they look upon the labor, and the wrought substance of them, 'See! this our fathers did for us.' "

PART TWO

Financing the New Church

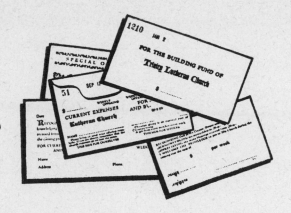

T H E   F I N A N C I A L   P L A N

Analyzing the Membership

In developing the financial plan the first step is to determine the financial resources of the congregation for the proposed task. A reliable estimate of the cost of the contemplated edifice must be secured. A good architect will be able to give this. Then a careful study must be made of the ability and willingness of the congregation to contribute. The committee must bracket the membership accordingly.

Suppose the goal is to raise about $40,000.00 in a congregation with approximately 250 prospective contributors. Suppose the plan adopted is to have payments made over a period of 18 months. The picture will look something like this:

5 pledges at $25.00 per month for 18 months ($450)	$ 2,250.00
5 pledges at $20.00 per month for 18 months ($360)	1,800.00
10 pledges at $15.00 per month for 18 months ($270)	2,700.00
150 pledges at $10.00 per month for 18 months ($180)	27,000.00
50 pledges at $ 5.00 per month for 18 months ($ 90)	4,500.00
30 pledges at $ 3.00 per month for 18 months ($ 54)	1,620.00
245	$40,820.00

One may say that it is easy to raise money on paper; but you must raise it on paper first. The potential financial strength of the congregation must be estimated in the light of what is known both of the ability and the willingness to give. Our Lord said if a man plans to build a tower he must first count the cost to see if he is able to complete the task.

The Installment Plan

The reasons for spreading the payments on building fund pledges over a longer period of time are quite obvious. Most folks receive their income in weekly, semi-monthly or monthly payments. The exception to this will be in rural districts where most of the cash is received when crops are sold. Not many folks can pay a pledge of this kind in one payment. The installment plan for paying pledges makes it easier for people to give more. Moreover, payments to contractors are made on a monthly basis. It is essential that payments on pledges be received as the cash is needed.

Payments may be made on a weekly, monthly or quarterly plan. For most contributors the weekly or monthly plan is best. Special envelopes should be provided for the purpose.

Over how long a period should payments be made? The writer has had experience with the one year, two year and three year plan. We recommend the eighteen month or two year plan, depending somewhat on the size of the project.

A four or five year plan is not good. Folks just will not start giving several years in advance of building operations. Besides, it is a universal experience that when a building is completed and taken into use payments on pledges fall off gradually. What has not been paid by the time the edifice is finished, or soon thereafter, very often never will be paid. It is so easy for folks to say, "We have the church now, and I think I need the money more than the congregation." There always will be some shrinkage of pledges made to any cause. The longer the period over which payments are to be made, the greater will be the shrinkage. So many things happen over a period of four or five years. Some members may move away and decide not to pay. Some die, which often means the pledge will not be paid. Some have financial reverses and cannot pay.

However, too much stress cannot be laid on the importance of having payments on pledges start a reasonable time *in advance of actual building operations.* It usually is difficult to get folks to see the need of this, but they must be made to see it. Here are the reasons for such advance payments: Most of the architect's fee must be paid by the time the contracts are let. Nearly all building contracts provide that 85% of the value of the work done and the materials delivered to the premises shall be paid at the end of each month. Invariably the payments during the first months of construction are very heavy. Excavation and pouring of footings and foundations does not take many weeks and this is a major part of the cost of the project. While this work is going on other materials are delivered to the premises. Hence cash has to be paid month by month in the early stages of the construction at a very rapid rate. Unless payments on subscriptions are started well in advance of building operations it will be necessary to borrow heavily during the period of construction. Such construction loans are not easy to get, and besides there is the interest to pay.

It usually takes from six months to a year to build a church, depending upon the size of the project, the availability of material and labor, and weather conditions. An ideal schedule will look something like this:

Term, 18 months.

Period of preparation for building fund campaign, February and March.

Canvass for pledges, in the month of May

Payments to begin, June 1

Building operations, to begin in May of the following year.

According to this schedule about two-thirds of the amount pledged will be in the treasury when construction begins and the final payment will be due by the time construction is completed. We know that the above schedule has been followed successfully.

Securing the Loan

Most churches are not able to raise the full amount of cash needed to complete their project; hence it becomes necessary to borrow. In analyzing the financial situation the committee must face these questions: How much will it be necessary to borrow; how much will the church be able to borrow; how much ought it to borrow?

No exact statement can be made as to the ratio which there ought to be between the amount to be borrowed and the value of the property. So much depends on the local situation. But, in general, it can be said that the debt ought not to be more than one-third of the value of the church and ground. Many finance companies will loan only up to one-fourth of the value of the property. None should loan more than fifty per cent of the value.

Having the architect's estimate of the cost of the project, the committee must carefully calculate the amount of cash that the congregation will raise by the time construction is completed. The difference between the estimated cost and the estimated income will be the amount to be borrowed. The next question then is, will the congregation be able to meet interest charges and prepayments? A plan for the amortization of the loan must be made. The contributions of individual members and the funds raised by auxiliary organizations of the congregation must provide the cash for interest and prepayments.

Before any contract is let two things must be done. First, the every-member canvass for pledges must be made. The response to this canvass is the real answer to the question: Shall we build a new church now? The other thing that must be done is to make the arrangements for a loan. We repeat, this must be done *before* contracts are let. Some churches have let contracts before being assured of a loan, with tragic results. Work had to stop even before the building was enclosed, involving much added expense and great embarrassment and sorrow for all concerned.

Church Extension Loans

Some congregations will seek church extension loans from the body with which they are affiliated. A church extension fund is a revolving fund which exists for the purpose of making loans for the construction or the purchase of churches and parsonages. However, a church extension loan, except in the case of small projects, usually is for secondary financing only. The congregation first raises all that it can from its membership; then it borrows as much as it can through a bond issue, or from some commercial lending institution. If it still lacks sufficient funds to proceed with the project it seeks a church extension loan. Such a loan, in general, is for this in-between financing, the amount that is lacking between what a congregation can raise from its members and the amount it can borrow through the usual channels.

Note: Congregations expecting to seek a church extension loan must bear in mind that the board administering this fund will require that the building plans as well as the financial plan be submitted to it for approval before a loan will be made.

What About Faith

What we have stated here about financial plans may seem like hard-boiled business. What about faith in God? Have not institutions and churches been built in ways that seemed not to be "good business principles" but in the faith that God would provide? This undoubtedly is true. In special cases, where there is a crying need, where one can be absolutely sure that God wills it, where there is no other way, we may confidently go forth, even though from a strictly business point of view we may seem to have no solid ground under our feet. If we know that God wants us to do it we may be sure that He will provide. But, normally, in the ordinary situation, where no emergency exists, we believe God expects us to use the good business sense which He has given us. Only then can we boldly ask Him to bless the undertaking and establish the work of our hand.

PREPARATION   AND   PROMOTION

From six weeks to two months will be required to prepare the congregation for a successful every-member canvass for building fund pledges. This means six weeks or two months prior to the canvass. The building fund committee (or the building committee acting in a dual capacity) must direct this work of preparation.

The canvassers should be selected early. If the membership is large the committee alone cannot make the every-member canvass. However, we doubt the wisdom of having too many solicitors. It is better to have a smaller group of carefully selected and well prepared canvassers. But select solicitors early. From the time one knows he is to help in the canvass of the membership he becomes doubly interested. Usually it is most effective to send out the canvassers in pairs.

Use of the Printed Word

Use the printed word. Usually three printed communications should be sent to the entire constituency of the congregation. The first may be just a brief statement announcing the undertaking and giving the plan in broad outline. This communication should give the dates of the special events in the promotional program as well as the dates for the actual canvass of the constituency.

The second and principal piece of printed matter to be used in this program of preparation should be a rather sizeable folder or small booklet. It should contain such things as: A picture of the proposed church, full information as to the estimated cost, the goal of the campaign for pledges and the details of the financial plan, a table showing how many pledges in various amounts will be required to reach the goal. There should be a stirring message from the pastor and brief endorsements of the projects by various officers of the congregation and members of the committee or committees. There may also be a message of encouragement from the church official who presides over the district, conference, synod or diocese. Money spent for an attractive, interesting and convincing folder of this kind will be money well spent.

If possible, a good slogan for the undertaking should be adopted and used in all printed matter.

The third piece of printed matter should be a brief final appeal telling of the progress made and asking all to cooperate with the solicitor.

It is obvious that if the church has a Sunday bulletin this should carry something about the task on every Sunday during the period of preparation and while the canvass is in progress.

The Spoken Word

Through the spoken word the cause should be presented in all auxiliary organizations, the women's societies, young people's societies, the brotherhood and the Sunday school. Some reference to the undertaking should be made at every worship service with a final sermon appropriate for the occasion on the last Sunday before the canvass begins.

Among texts suitable for such a sermon are: Neh. 4:6, Ps. 90:16-17, Ps. 84, Ps. 27:4, Matt. 26:6-13, Matt. 18:20, Ephes. 2:20, I Cor. 13:1-3; II Cor. 9:6-8.

There should be a great rally of young and old just before the canvass begins. At this rally it may be well to have a guest speaker for the main address, one who can help to put the congregation in heart and spirit for the supreme effort which is about to be made. There should be a number of four-minute pep talks by members of the committee, officers of the church and its organizations and a few others. Then, a brief final word from the pastor.

There should be no soliciting of pledges at this rally. It should be so announced. Avoid, if possible, having anyone get up in the meeting to say: "I'll give $100," or some other amount. The danger is that such an offer will be far out of line. For if the first subscriptions made are too low there is great probability that the whole campaign will be a failure. It is like giving the pitch to the choir: If you pitch the sopranos too low, all the other parts will be pitched too low. People ought not to look so much at what others are giving when they are asked to contribute. But they often do. We know of a prosperous church where the wealthiest man in the congregation started things by announcing in a meeting that he would give $500. He ought to have given at least four times as much. But this set the pace for the rest of the membership. The whole subscription effort proved a disappointment. The result has been that the congregation has been carrying a very large load of debt through many years.

On the final Sunday before the general solicitation begins there should be a consecration service for the canvassers. They are going out to do holy work. They should be commissioned in a worthy way. Such a consecration service will help to put the whole enterprise on a high spiritual plane.

The Pre-canvass

There should always be a pre-canvass of a few of the members. This is to insure a right start. So much depends on a good start. Some must set the pace. There are good souls in most every congregation that always can be counted on to do the generous thing. These need not be the most prosperous. But if their pledges be generous in view of their circumstances they will serve the purpose of the pre-canvass. Usually this pre-canvass of a few members should be made by the pastor in company with a member or two of the committee. The result of the pre-canvass should be announced at the rally. In a campaign in a church served by the writer we were able to announce at the rally that already $30,000.00 had been subscribed by a relatively small number of members. This announcement made the success of the canvass which followed a certainty.

Instructing the Solicitors

There must be at least one good meeting of the canvassers before the general solicitation begins. Here the names of those to be seen by each team must be assigned and a sufficient number of pledge cards or blanks must be distributed to the workers and final instructions given. While no quota should be given for each person to be solicited, the canvassers must have some general idea as to the amount it is hoped to receive from each prospect. Above all it must be impressed on the solicitors that to reach the goal set by the congregation will require that a certain average be maintained. To reach this some will have to give much more than the average, because always there are some who give less. A table should be placed before the canvassers, perhaps on a blackboard, showing how many subscriptions will be required in each bracketed amount in order to reach the goal which has been set. In every case the prospect should be asked how much he will give *per month* (or per week) for the specified length of time during which payments are to be made.

The following form of pledge may be used:

TRINITY LUTHERAN CHURCH

Chicago, Ill. _____ 19____ $_____

    For the purpose of creating a building fund for the erection of a church edifice for Trinity Lutheran Church, Chicago, Illinois, and in consideration of the gifts by others to the said building fund, I promise to pay to Trinity Lutheran Church, Chicago, Illinois, or its order, the sum of _____ dollars, payable as follows: $_____ on or before _____ and the balance in equal monthly installments until paid in full.

_____
Signature

_____
Address

It should be noted that the words "and in consideration of gifts by others," and so forth, are important legally.

A good type of blank is one in which there is a carbon copy duplicate. The stub of the pledge blank should have a complete record of the pledge. The duplicate of the pledge should be given to the contributor. The person making the pledge should himself sign the blank.

Two weeks should be set aside for canvassing the constituency. The solicitors should report the result of their work daily to the chairman of the committee or to the captain of the group to which the team belongs.

Keeping on a High Spiritual Level

The appeal for contributions should be put on a high spiritual plane. There should be a constant aim to make the task of spiritual benefit to the congregation. The people should be exhorted first to give themselves to the Lord and then a portion of their means. There is much spiritual beauty in an undertaking of this kind if it is properly directed and promoted. It offers a great opportunity to teach true stewardship. There will be need of much prayer. "Unless the Lord build the temple they labor in vain who build thereon." Motives must be kept pure. "Though I give my body to be burned and have not love, it profiteth me nothing." The dynamic must be love to God, gratitude for His countless mercies and love of the church.

Sacrificial Giving

There will be need of sacrifice. The people must be made to realize that with rare exceptions it is through sacrifice that churches have been built. Folks must be willing to do without certain things that the House of God may be built. Many strange things are built into the foundations and walls of churches: Hats and gowns and suits and coats that never were bought. Furniture and rugs that folks decided to do without. Vacation trips that were not taken. All this in order that there might be more to give for the building of the Lord's House. In this way the people are building something of their very selves into the structure.

The writer has seen folks go without even necessities that they might have a little to give for the church. One young woman working for a very small wage decided to give up her usual cup of coffee at noon in order that she might save five cents per day for her building fund pledge.

The hard way, the way of sacrifice, is the best way to get a church, for "where your treasure is there your heart is also." In this way the greatest spiritual blessing will come back to the congregation, for "he that soweth sparingly shall reap also sparingly and he that soweth bountifully shall reap bountifully, . . . for God loveth a cheerful giver." II Cor. 9:7.

Let us not hesitate to encourage people to give liberally for the Kingdom of God, even unto sacrifice. To be sure, the Bible stresses free-will giving. But it also stresses liberal giving and it bids us "provoke one another to love and good works." Heb. 10:24.

Memorials and Special Gifts

The solicitation of memorials and special gifts should wait until the entire constituency has been canvassed for the regular building fund subscriptions, in fact, until the major portion of the pledge made has been paid. The matter of supreme importance is to get the building itself. You can take years, if necessary, to get the equipment. This saves interest and keeps the membership working.

At the right time list the special gifts which are desired. Among these will be included: Windows, pulpit, altar, font, cross, candlesticks, altar vestments, offering plates, lectern, hymn books, pipe organ, outside bulletin board. These may be given by organizations within the congregation as well as by individuals and families. Such special gifts usually come very easily after the church has been built and the regular building fund pledge has been paid, or nearly so.

Windows should be double glazed, having an outside protection glass and an inside groove for the stained glass. Then if there is not sufficient cash for the purchase of art windows when the building is completed these can easily be added later. Double glazing is an advantage aside from the reason for it given here. The stained glass is protected, "sweating" is prevented, and the building made more comfortable, both in summer and in winter.

Professional Campaign Directors

A word might be in order here about professional campaign directors. Many of these unquestionably are both competent and trustworthy and are highly recommended by those who have used them. But there is nothing very mysterious about the technique of a building fund campaign. If the procedures outlined here, adapted, of course, to local circumstances, are followed, it should be possible to have a very efficient and successful campaign. The pastor is the key man in such an effort, as in most everything else that is undertaken in the church. He must furnish the inspiration, the guidance, and generate the enthusiasm. Relying on the pastor and one's home forces to direct the work has the added advantage that you do not have to pay extra for it.

Collections

In concluding this discussion of the financial plans we want to say a word about collections. There have been many fine campaigns for pledges that were not followed by an efficient plan for collections. A pledge has no value until it is paid. As already stated, special envelopes should be provided, monthly or weekly. The returns should be watched closely. If the promised payment is not received quite promptly a reminder by mail, by telephone or personal call should be given. This will be the responsibility of the committee. But this important part of the task must be efficiently organized. *The success of the whole enterprise hinges on the collections.* Most serious attention must be given to this matter. A good slogan to use here is: "It is easier to keep up than to catch up."

There are other ways of doing this. Bethel Lutheran Church in Madison, Wisconsin, raised over $50,000.00 in three great Easter offerings. Of course, these offerings were preceded by a great deal of careful and prayerful preparation. Any system is good if it works. But, in general, a monthly or weekly envelope system for paying building fund pledges works the best.

Conclusion

"Rise up and build!" "Except the Lord build the Temple they labor in vain who build thereon." As you build may the prayer of Moses ever be in your heart: "Let the beauty of the Lord our God be upon us; and establish thou the work of our hands upon us; yea, the work of our hands establish thou it."

"Take heed now for the Lord hath chosen thee to build a house for the sanctuary, be strong and do it." II Chron. 28:10.

PART THREE

Model Churches

GOTHIC

Grace Lutheran Church, Detroit, Michigan. Fichter and Brooker, Architects.
An excellent example of a Gothic Church with tower at the crossing of the
nave and transepts

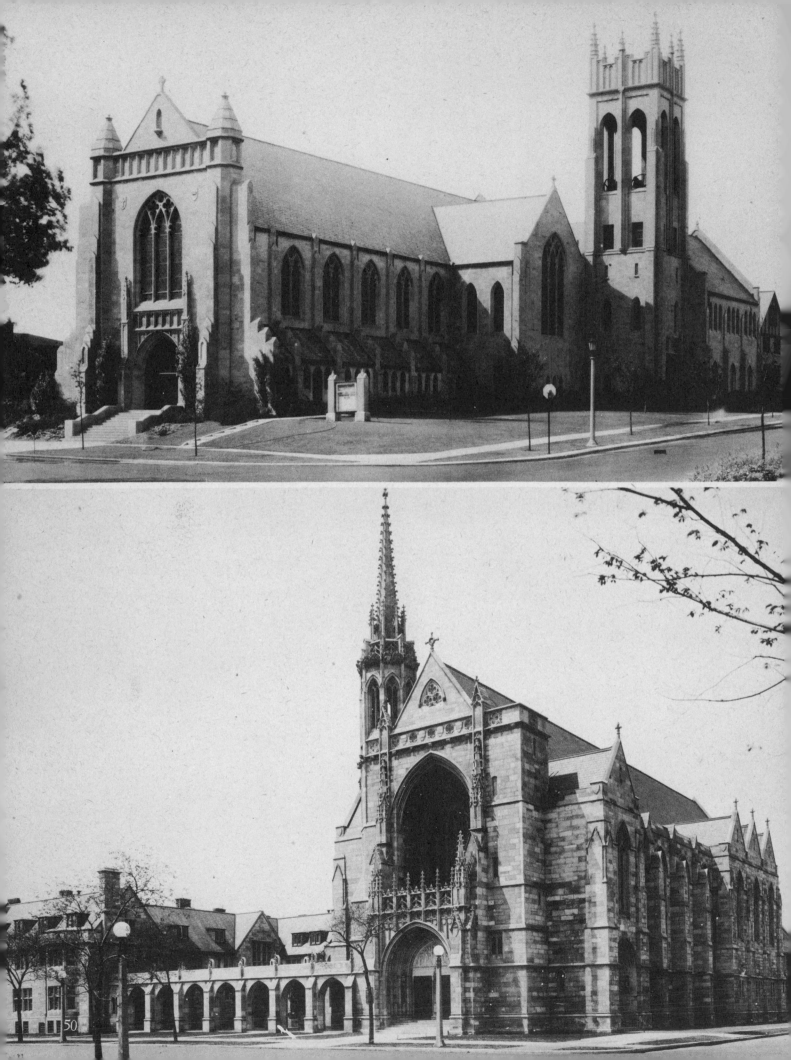

Left above:

United Lutheran Church parish house and parsonage, Oak Park, Illinois. Herbert A. Brand, Architect

Left below:

Fourth Presbyterian Church, Chicago. Cram, Goodhue and Ferguson, Architects. Howard Shaw, Associate. One of the finest examples of Gothic architecture

Right above:

Grace Lutheran Church, River Forest, Illinois. Talmadge and Watson, Architects. This is Gothic somewhat in the modern spirit

Right below:

Salem Lutheran Church and parish house, Chicago. Hanson and Associates, Architects, formerly Polson and Hanson and Associates

Bethlehem Lutheran Church, Baldwin, Long Island, New York.
Cherry and Matz, Architects. First unit built in 1943

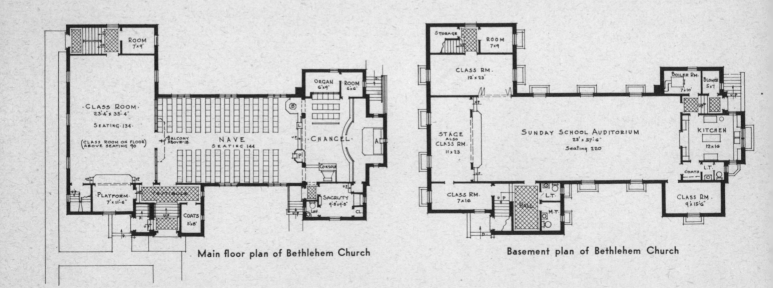

Main floor plan of Bethlehem Church

Basement plan of Bethlehem Church

COVER—DESIGN FOR MEDILL AVENUE LUTHERAN CHURCH, CHICAGO

H. C. HEUSER, ARCHITECT

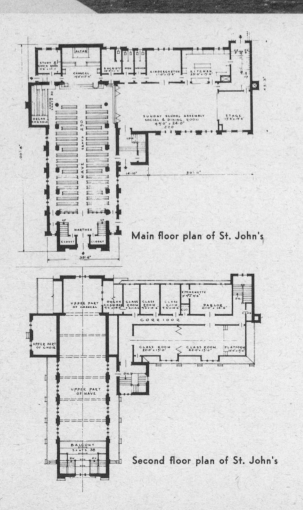

Main floor plan of St. John's

Second floor plan of St. John's

Interior of St. John's

St. John's Lutheran Church, Sycamore, Illinois.
Herbert A. Brand, Architect

Immanuel Lutheran Church, Forest City, Iowa. Thorwald Thorson, Architect. This is Gothic with details slightly towards the modern expression

Interior of Immanuel

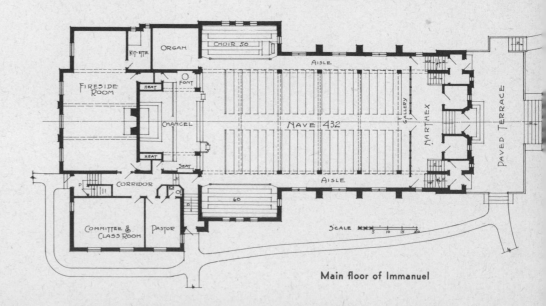

Main floor of Immanuel

First Congregational Church, Highland, Illinois.
Herbert A. Brand, Architect

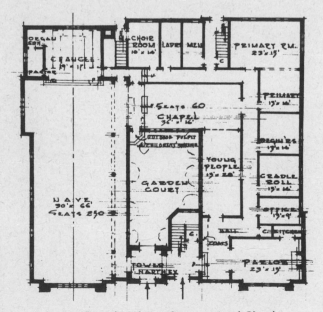

Main floor plan of First Congregational Church

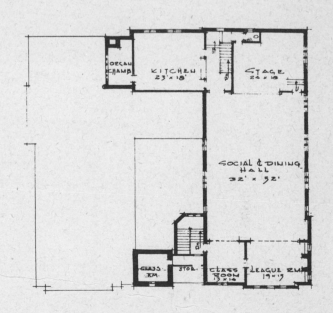

Second floor plan of First Congregational Church

Chancel of First Lutheran Church, Albert Lea, Minnesota. Slifer and Abrahamson, Architects

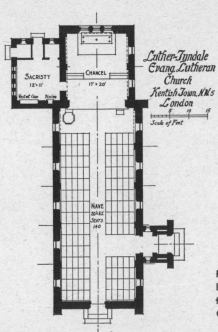

Floor plan of Luther-Tyndale. Indicates the proper proportion of length to width in a Gothic Church

Chancel of Luther-Tyndale Lutheran Church, Kentish Town, N. W., London

BYZANTINE

Ascension Church, Roman Catholic, Oak Park, Illinois. Meyer and Cook, Architects. An example of Byzantine

R O M A N E S Q U E

St. Vincent De Paul Roman Catholic Church, Chicago.
An excellent example of Romanesque

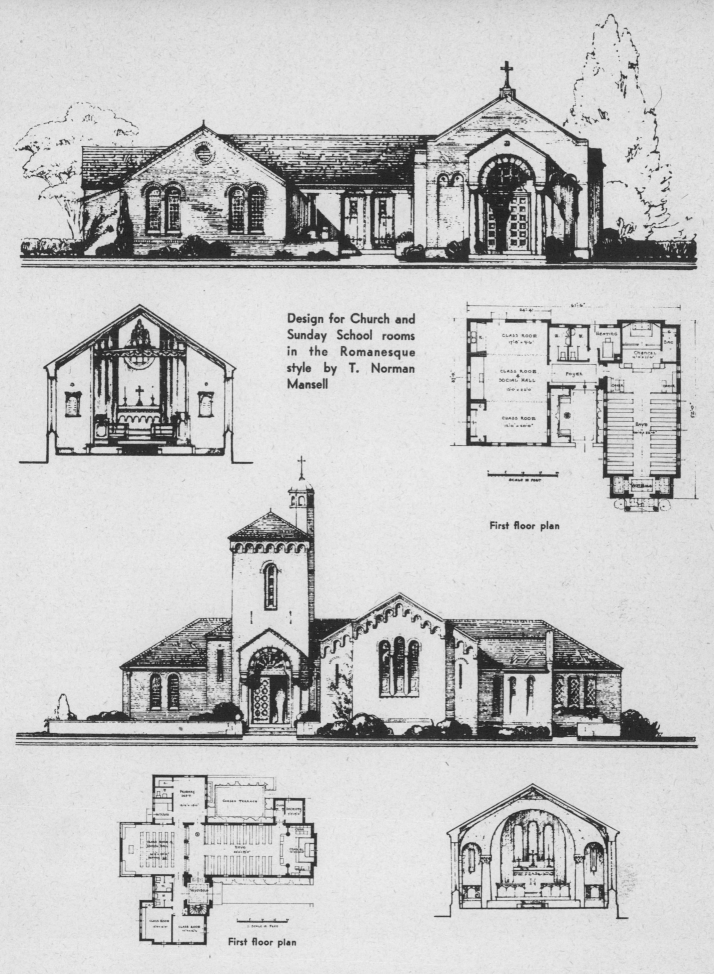

Design for Church and Sunday School rooms in the Romanesque style by T. Norman Mansell

First floor plan

First floor plan

Design for Church and Parish House in the Romanesque style. T. Norman Mansell, Architect

COLONIAL

St. Bartholomew Roman Catholic Church, Chicago.
Gerald Barry, Architect. Seating Capacity, 1,200

Above:

Good Shepherd Lutheran Church, Oak Park, Illinois.
Hotchkiss and Bird, Architects. An example of a small
brick Colonial Church

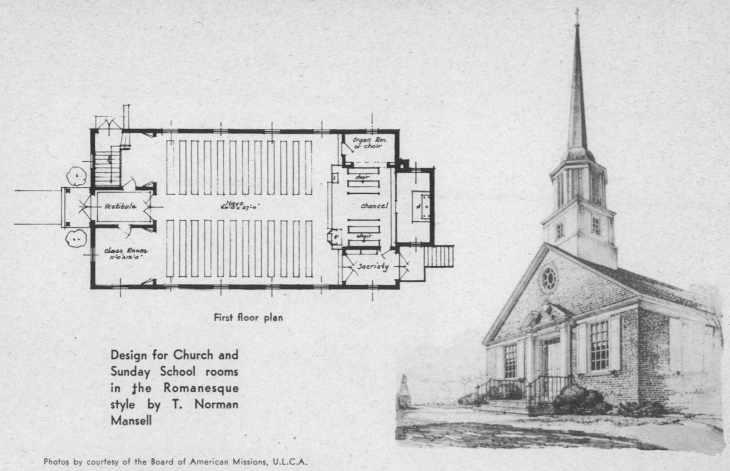

First floor plan

Design for Church and
Sunday School rooms
in the Romanesque
style by T. Norman
Mansell

Community Baptist Church, Warrenville, Illinois. Herbert A. Brand, Architect

Immaculate Conception Church, Roman Catholic, Mundelein, Illinois

Interior of Methodist Church, Woodside, Maryland. Wenner and Fink, Architects. Photo by courtesy Inter-denominational Architectural Bureau, New York, E. M. Conover, director

Projected church and community house in colonial design. Edward F. Jansson, Architect, Frank L. Venning, Associate, Chicago

MODERN

Memorial Lutheran Church, Pierre, South Dakota. Thorwald Thorson, Architect. The design is modern but the layout is traditional

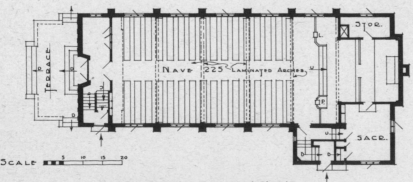

Main floor plan of Memorial Church

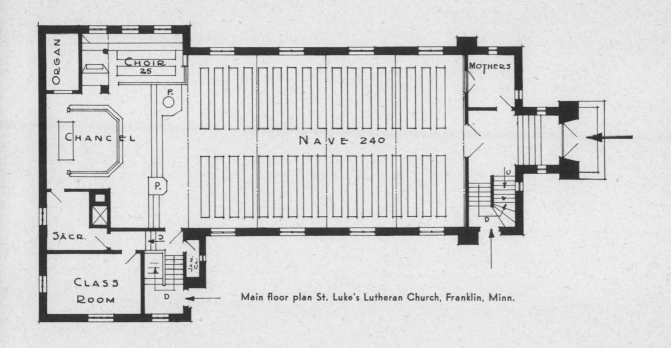

Main floor plan St. Luke's Lutheran Church, Franklin, Minn.

St. Luke's Lutheran Church, Franklin, Minnesota.
Thorwald Thorson, architect

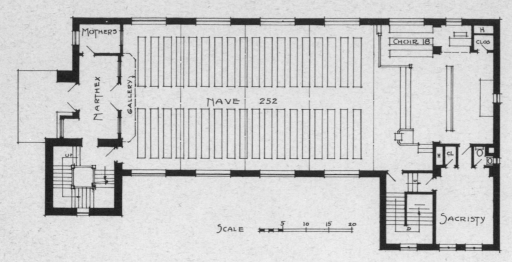

Main floor plan of Trinity Church

Trinity Lutheran Church, Rhinelander, Wisconsin. Thorwald Thorson, Architect. The walls are of ordinary field stone, usually called "niggerheads." This is an excellent material which is obtainable in many communities

First Lutheran Church, Clarion, Iowa. Thorwald Thorson, architect. This church is designed in the modern spirit but has the traditional layout. The exterior is finished in redwood in a natural wood oil finish

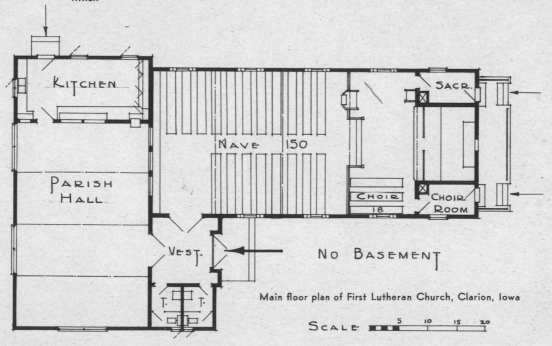

KITCHEN

PARISH HALL

NAVE 150

SACR.

CHOIR 18

CHOIR ROOM

VEST.

NO BASEMENT

T. T.

Main floor plan of First Lutheran Church, Clarion, Iowa

SCALE   5   10   15   20

THE SMALL FRAME CHURCH

Grace Lutheran Church, Teaneck, New Jersey. Harold C. Bernhard, Architect. A beautiful example of a small frame church

Interior of Grace Church

Calvary Lutheran Church, Leonia, New Jersey. Harold C. Bernhard, Architect. An inexpensive frame church of good design

St. Rita's Roman Catholic Church, Solon, Ohio. Joseph J. Stock, Architect. A charming example of a small frame church

St. Hubert's Roman Catholic Church, near Kirtland, Ohio. Edward G. Reed, Architect. A good example of a small frame church

Breckenridge Lutheran Church, Breckenridge, Minnesota. N. Edward Mohn, Architect. A good example of a medium size frame church. Seating capacity in the nave, 235.

SPANISH

First Lutheran Church, Pasadena, California. Kennedy and Ogilvie, Architects. A good example of a design appropriate for those sections of the country to which this type of architecture is native

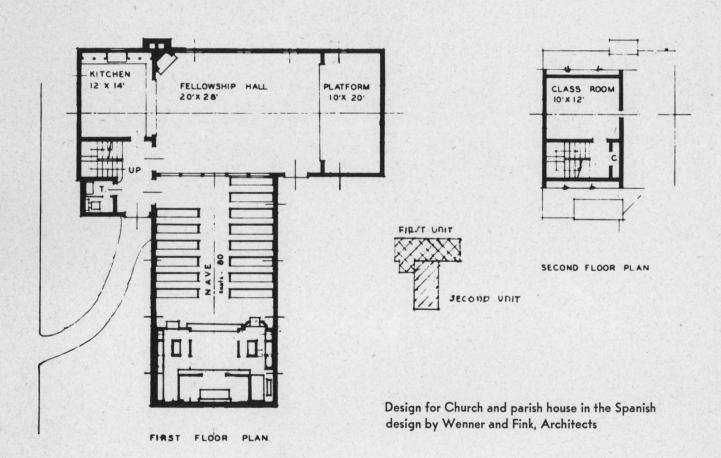

KITCHEN
12' X 14'

FELLOWSHIP HALL
20' X 28'

PLATFORM
10' X 20'

UP

T.

NAVE
Seats 80

FIRST FLOOR PLAN

CLASS ROOM
10' X 12'

C

SECOND FLOOR PLAN

FIRST UNIT

SECOND UNIT

Design for Church and parish house in the Spanish
design by Wenner and Fink, Architects

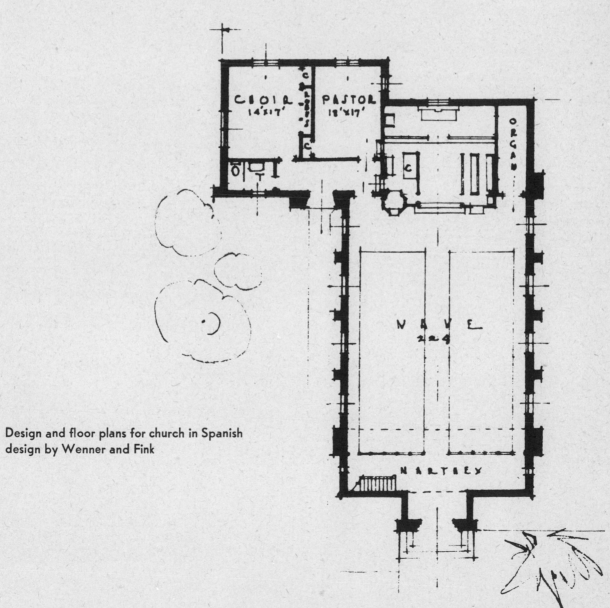

Design and floor plans for church in Spanish
design by Wenner and Fink

LOG CHURCHES

Grace Lutheran Church, near McGregor, Minnesota. An example of the fine results that can be attained by using the materials which are near at hand

Interior of Grace Church

Calvary Lutheran Church, Minong, Wisconsin. This church was built of cement blocks with field stone foundation at a very low cost

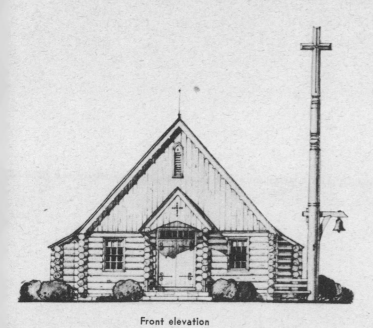

Front elevation

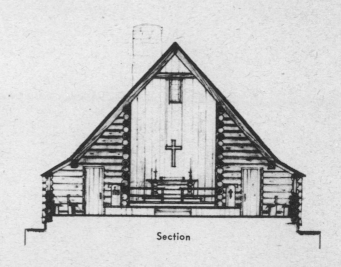

Section

Side elevation

Log church designed by T. Norman Mansell

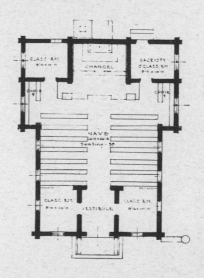

Floor plan

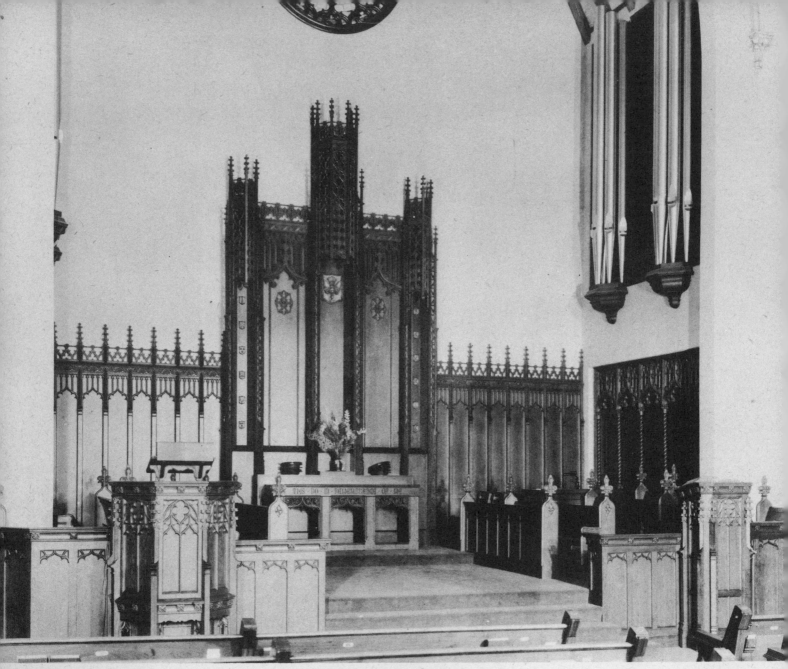

Interior of First Presbyterian Church, Topeka, Kansas, after remodeling

REMODELED INTERIORS

Interior of First Presbyterian Church, Topeka, Kansas, before remodeling

First Presbyterian Church, Springfield, Illinois, after remodeling. Interior redesigned by Edward F. Jansson and Frank L. Vening.

First Presbyterian Church, Springfield, Illinois, before remodelling

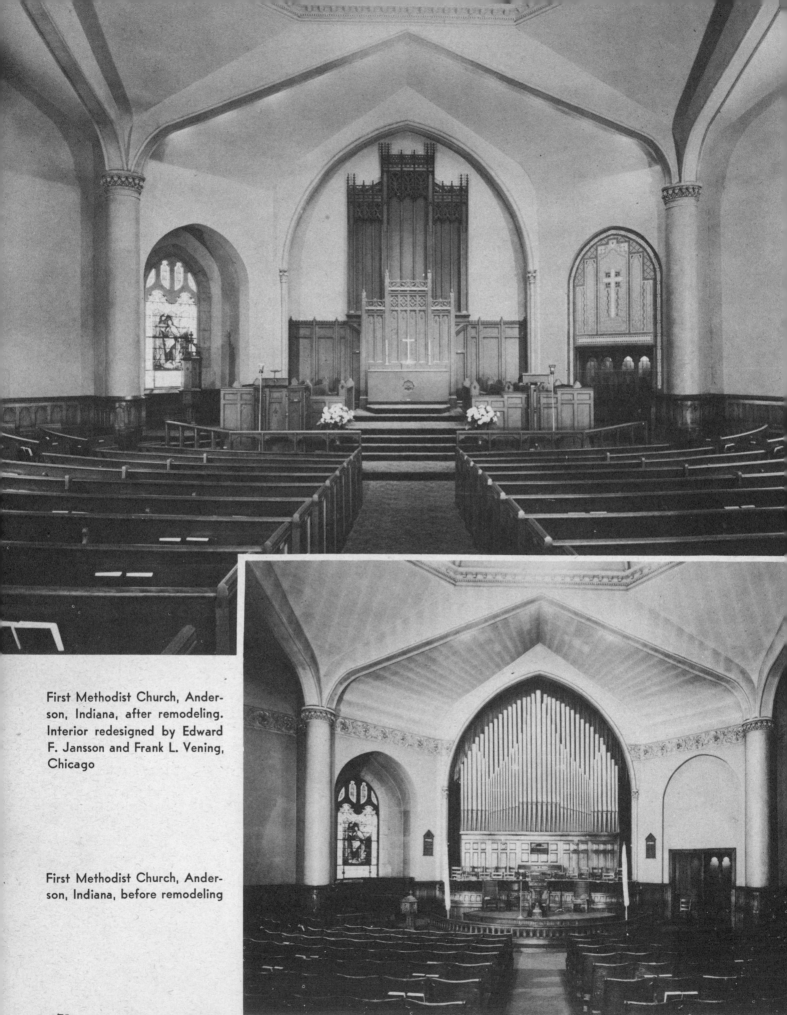

First Methodist Church, Anderson, Indiana, after remodeling. Interior redesigned by Edward F. Jansson and Frank L. Vening, Chicago

First Methodist Church, Anderson, Indiana, before remodeling

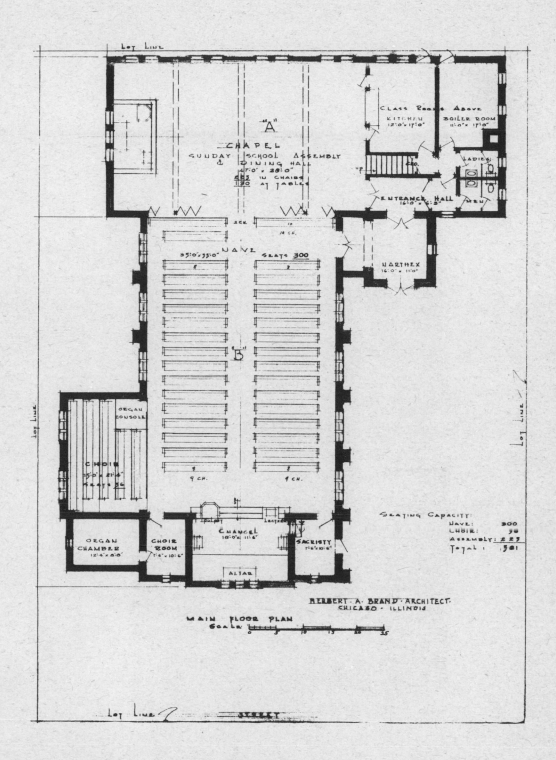

A floor plan by Herbert A. Brand. This shows how a parish house can be made to add seating for overflow attendance.

BIBLIOGRAPHY

The writer will make but two suggestions as to books that will be helpful for those who are interested in church architecture. First we recommend *Church Building,* by Ralph Adams Cram. Mr. Cram is one of the world's greatest authorities on Gothic churches. Anyone having to do with planning a church ought to read at least this one of Mr. Cram's books.

The second book which we recommend is *The Small Church, How to Build and Furnish It,* by F. R. Webber. The author is a pastor as well as an architect and engineer. For a time he was associated with Mr. Cram. This volume contains twenty chapters, covering practically every phase of the task of planning and furnishing a church. There are 270 illustrations. There is a bibliography which lists 74 books covering the field of ecclesiastical art and architecture. Mr. Webber's book will be found to be of inestimable value. *Church Symbolism,* by the same author, is another book of great value for those who have to do with planning and furnishing a church.